J.O.U.R.N.A.L

A GUIDE TO MENTAL HEALTH

JOURNEY OF OPTIMISM, UNDERSTANDING,
REFLECTION, NURTURING, ACCEPTANCE, AND LOVE

Dr. Katherine Y. Brown

www.TrueVinePublishing.org

JOURNAL: A Guide to Mental Health
Dr. Katherine Y. Brown

Published by
True Vine Publishing Co.
810 Dominican Dr.
Nashville, TN 37228
www.TrueVinePublishing.org

ISBN: 978-1-962783-03-3 Paperback
ISBN: 978-1-962783-04-0 eBook

Printed in the United States of America—First Print

Dedication

This book is dedicated to everyone on their journey of self-discovery, whether you are in moments of clarity or navigating through tough times as you grow and change. Your feelings are important, your experiences are real, and your mental health matters. This guide is here to help you find ways to inspire deeper reflection and encourage you to care for, accept, and love yourself. Always remember: you're not alone.

Setting the Stage With Reflections of Hope

The foundation of healthcare is emphasized by one pivotal word: care. As a nurse, I've witnessed the profound importance of holistic well-being, which includes both mind and body. This book offers a variety of concepts and examples to guide you in placing yourself at the forefront. Make your well-being the top priority.

—Anthony D. Rodgers, LPN

As a current medical student at Charles R. Drew University College of Medicine and Science, I cannot emphasize enough the importance of mental health. The reality is crystal clear: mental health is just as important as physical health. With the countless demands of our daily lives, understanding that mental well-being is integral to comprehensive health is essential for the quality of life. As you progress through the pages of this book, let it serve as a reminder to pause, breathe, reflect, and nourish your inner self. You are worth it.

—Student Doctor Sydney Y.K. Brown, M.A., B.S

Mental health knows no gender. It's a universal aspect of our existence, impacting every individual regardless of their identity. It's imperative to seek and find coping mechanisms that resonate with you–be it exercise, journaling, music, or any other therapeutic outlet. Discover what helps you thrive, for your well-being is important, and always remember: you matter.

—Irving D. Brown III, B.S

In a world where we talk about almost everything, isn't it time we included our mental health in the conversation? No matter if you are entering childhood, teenage years, or navigating the complexities of adulthood, conversations about mental well-being deserve attention and a seat at the table. Let's ensure that health, in all its forms, is part of our everyday life.

—Robert D. Brown

Acknowledgments

I would like to thank everyone who has contributed to this work. This began from a conversation and grew into something much bigger. There are reflections shared that came from amazing individuals willing to lend their voices and join a collective conversation. This is a testament to the power of WE and unity. There is sincere gratitude for the contributors who shared their insights in this book: Anthony D. Rodgers, LPN; Student Doctor Sydney Y. K. Brown, MA, BS; Irving D. Brown, BS; Robert D. Brown; Kimberlee Wyche Etheridge, MD, MPH; Bailee Smith; Delnita Smith; Saidia Bell; Zeboreh Bynum; Trenay Perry Bynum, MSP; Lillian Floyd-Thomas; Cydney Elliott; TiNiah Abernathy; Amara King; Alivia K. Dove; Lauryn Smith; and Hallie Sheffield. Words cannot express my profound thanks to all of you and everyone who made this possible.

Table of Contents

Preface

Growing up, we used to play a funny joke on our unsuspecting classmates, either on the school bus or in the schoolyard. Someone would say, "I see your epidermis!" The person would look confused and unsure of what was going on. They would start looking around and checking themselves for flaws, thinking something must be wrong. Others would join in, talking about the visibility of the epidermis. Eventually, after some friendly laughter, the person would catch on that the epidermis was just a fancy word for their skin. It suddenly made sense – we all have it. Our skin covers and protects us, but it rarely reveals much about what's happening inside.

Similarly, we all have mental health. Like our skin, it's one of the first things people notice about us. Our mood, our energy levels, how engaged or disengaged we seem – all of these are ways our mental health manifests itself. But just like with our skin, what's on the surface doesn't tell our whole story. It doesn't show the many layers that make each of us who we are.

This book is a guide to help each person discover what's inside; it's a journey of self-discovery. We're not the same as we were yesterday, and we won't be the same tomorrow. How we interact with the world teaches us important lessons about ourselves. How we react to our daily experiences shapes our growing brain and influences how we respond to similar situations in the future. Some lessons are positive, others are negative, but they all come together to shape who we are. The second decade of life (ages 10-20) is a time of wonder and transformation. Growth, both physical and mental, speeds along for everyone.

The third decade and beyond build on these early years, setting the stage for mental health throughout our lives. Knowing you're not alone on this journey, that others are walking the same path, makes it all feel more normal. The people who shared their stories for this book did so because they believed that something they went through might help someone else. From the caterpillar, the butterfly emerges. No two are the same, but all have gone through the same process of growing up. Think of this book as your field guide, and appreciate the uniqueness and openness of the individuals who shared their stories and the self-discovery it makes possible.

-Kimberlee Wyche Etheridge, MD, MPH

Introduction

Welcome to *Journal: A Guide to Mental Health,* your personal toolkit filled with practical, powerful, and transformative tips to support your mental well-being. Throughout the book, there are places where the word journal is used creatively as an acronym: J.O.U.R.N.A.L: Journey of Optimism, Understanding, Reflection, Nurturing, Acceptance, and Love. There is an emphasis on the importance of journaling.

The years of your life can shift from being exciting and dynamic to becoming some of the most challenging. With transitions, growth spurts, academic and professional pressures, changing relationships, and the search for identity–not to mention the many different emotions–it can all feel a bit overwhelming at times.

The saying, "Mental health is **health**" holds great importance. There are times when gatherings such as a block party serves two purposes—one to just have fun and the other for a time for relaxation, fellowship and creating positive environments. You'll read more about this in the chapter on "Lessons Learned from a Block Party." Just as our physical well-being is crucial to out overall health, our psychological state is an equally vital role in our quality of life. Neither aspect of health outweighs the other; both are integral to our overall well-being. And that's where J.O.U.R.N.A.L comes in.

This journal will provide you with 101 straightforward, effective tips to guide you on this journey. I encourage you to take **10 minutes** out of your day to reflect and write.

J.O.U.R.N.A.L isn't just about putting words on paper. It's about self-discovery. It's about becoming the best version of yourself. Let's begin.

Beginning the Journey

I remember the day a 9-year-old girl named Bailee attended her first session at the Dr. Katherine Y. Brown (KYB) Leadership Academy in Nashville, Tennessee. It was a sunny Sunday in August 2023, and the bright sun outside seemed completely at odds with the storm of emotions swirling inside the car parked outside the academy. Inside the car, Bailee sat, tears streaming down her face, filled with fear about stepping out into the unknown. Her mother, a mixture of concerned and encouraging, gently urged her to give it a try. But Bailee remained trapped in her fears and uncertainties.

After what felt like an eternity, Bailee finally took a deep breath, wiped away her tears, and summoned the courage to open the car door. Her small feet touched the ground, and she took hesitant steps, one after the other, until she made her way inside the building.

Later that day, in a quiet moment with her mother, Bailee asked, "Mom, do you ever feel like crying like I did?" Her mother, with all the wisdom and compassion of her years, simply replied, "Yes."

On that day, Bailee began to grasp not just the meaning of the acronym J.O.U.R.N.A.L, but also the profound importance of mental health. She realized that emotions, understanding them, and confronting fears weren't concepts reserved for adults alone. They were universal, bridging the gap between a child's innocent tears and an adult's silent struggles.

Bailee's journey, while unique in its details, carries a universal essence. It serves as a testament to the significance of mental health at all ages. It's about facing fears head-on, comprehending our emotions, and discovering that courage can be found in the most unexpected places – sometimes, right in the backseat of a car on a sunny day.

To readers, young and old, this book serves as a reminder that understanding ourselves is the first step toward healing and growth. Embrace the journey.

Dear Reader,

Hi, my name is Bailee. I'm 9 years old, and I wanted to share a little bit about a big day in my life. You see, there was this one day when I felt a whole bunch of feelings all jumbled up inside me. It was my first day at the KYB Leadership Academy, and I felt like a tiny fish in a huge pond.

My mom drove me there, and even though the sun was shining outside, it felt like there was a storm inside my heart. I was so scared! I sat in our car and cried. My tummy felt all funny, and I didn't want to go inside. What if I didn't make any friends? What if it was too hard?

But then, something my mom said made me think. I asked her if she ever felt like crying like I did. And you know what? She said she did. That made me think. If my mom, who's the strongest person I know, feels like this sometimes, maybe it's okay that I do too.

So, I decided to be brave. I wiped my tears, got out of the car, and took a deep breath. And guess what? It wasn't as scary as I thought. Plus, I got to learn about J.O.U.R.N.A.L and how important it is to understand our feelings and talk about them.

I wanted to share my story with you because maybe you've felt scared or nervous like I did. And I want you to know that it's okay. It's okay to feel things and to talk about them. We're all on a journey, and sometimes, it's good to have a little help along the way.

Hey there,

I'm Delnita, but most folks around here just call me Bailee's mom. The first time Bailee went to KYB Leadership Academy, my heart was all over the place. I couldn't stop thinking about my youngest, my baby, going into a room of teens to learn about leadership. Yeah, she is used to working with teens and she does get a little more attention than my other kiddos. That day, all the kids had on black shoes, but not Bailee. She was dead set on wearing her pink sandals. Part of me wondered, should I make her wear the black shoes like everyone else or let her be her own person?

But then, right in the middle of one of those leadership sessions, Bailee came over, staying close and hugging me. Without thinking, I gave her a kiss, right then and there. Maybe it was just a mom being a mom, but in that moment, surrounded by her peers, I wondered if I'd made a mistake. Dr. Katherine saw it too and had a quiet chat with Bailee about how some things, even nice things, can make others feel a bit left out.

Later on, during another part of the training when I leaned in for another goodbye kiss, Bailee stopped me. She had this big, proud smile and said we should think about the other kids who don't get kisses from their moms during our trainings. I was stunned! In that little moment, my Bailee seemed so much older and wiser.

She later told me that the one word she'd use to describe her day was "love." And you know what? That's what it's all about. It's not just the love between a mom and her kid, but the bigger kind of love that looks out for everyone.

Writing this down, thinking about it, it's made me see that every day's a lesson. For me, for Bailee, for all of us.

Thanks for reading our story,
Delnita.

◌

Every life has moments that define it, where our emotions guide our actions and teach us lessons. Bailee's story, interwoven with her mother's, is a single thread in the tapestry of the human experience. These are just a few of the experiences that motivated me to write this book for you. I've crafted the J.O.U.R.N.A.L to be your companion, your guide, in reflecting on your own emotions and experiences.

Each of the seven major themes in this book represents a critical aspect of your journey toward improved mental health. When you consider the concept of journaling, a journal isn't simply a tool for writing; rather, it's a roadmap for self-discovery, symbolizing a Journey, Optimism, Understanding, Reflection, Nurturing, Acceptance, and Love. These words have significance:

J - Journey

Think of life like a long road trip. Some days are smooth, and others have bumps. There might be days when the path seems unclear, and you're unsure where you're heading. But always remember, it's about moving forward, taking things one step at a time, and enjoying the ride.

O - Optimism

How you think about things can change everything. For instance, when it rains on a day you want to go out, you can see it as a ruined day or a chance to enjoy a cozy moment indoors. You can also view the rain as a positive that replenishes the flowers and nature. It's about looking for the good side, even when things don't go as planned. Keeping a hopeful and positive attitude can turn challenges into opportunities.

U - Understanding

Knowing how you feel is a big part of life. Sometimes you might be happy, sometimes sad, and sometimes confused. And that's okay. It's essential to think about why you feel a certain way and to try and understand those around you too.

R - Reflection

Everyone needs some time to think. It's like when you sit by a window and watch the world outside. Think about your day, what went well, and what you'd like to change. This quiet thinking time helps you learn and grow.

N - Nurturing

Imagine if you had a small plant. It would need water, sunlight, and care to grow. You're a bit like that plant. You need good food, rest, and fun times to be your best self.

A - Acceptance

Sometimes, things don't go as planned. Maybe it rains on your picnic day or your ice cream falls on the ground. It's okay to be sad, but it's also essential to accept things and move on. Life's full of surprises, and not all of them are fun, but they're all part of the story.

L - Love

Everyone needs some form of love. It's like a warm hug on a cold day. Remember to be kind to yourself, like being your own best friend. And spread some of that love and kindness to others; it makes everyone feel good.

Every individual has preferred methods to reflect and even to cope with and adapt to unfamiliar circumstances. Some find enjoyment in art, some in music, and others in the written word. The impact of journaling, in particular, can offer a great tool for introspection, growth, and reflection. Let me introduce you to Saidia Bell. Her journey with journaling, as a member of the KYB Leadership Academy Cohort 4 gives a great example of learning the power of journaling.

Saidia Bell - KYB Leadership Academy Cohort 4
Senior College Student at Tennessee State University

Saidia explains:

Writing in a journal is extremely personal and helpful when dealing with new environments and new endeavors. It allows you to document what's happening in your life and around you. I'd like to talk about a time when journaling was my savior and number one friend. I've been a part of KYB Leadership Academy since I was a junior in high school. The academy helped mold me into the leader that I am today by showing me how to talk to people and represent myself. Therefore, I'm forever grateful for the opportunities made possible with my membership. In addition, I had the chance to travel to Medellin, Colombia for the first time in 2016. There I had a lot of fun but struggled when it came to building relationships and friendships due to me not having either of my sisters who were a part of my cohort with me. Consequently, once it was brought to my attention by one of the other students that I wasn't being approachable I began to journal.

I would not only vlog (create videos) but I'd write in a journal as well. Majority of the time I would write alone outside or alone listening to music or nature to ground me before I'd go into detail about the day or night that had passed.

Journaling was my safe place because I was able to sit with my thoughts unbothered and write about my experience away from home and away from my family for the first and the longest time. Moreover, once I got a little older I noticed how since that initial experience with KYB writing has always been a positive coping mechanism for me when it comes to dealing with stressful environments because it gives me a break from reality. As a result, I consider vlogging and journaling while in school is extremely important because it allows you to voice your opinion and emotions in a light where no one can ridicule them. It allows you to think outside the box and open up without the distractions of sidebar annotations and connotations and for that I loved every bit of my first global leadership opportunity.

೪

Saidia embraced something new and had the courage to find a new place of peace in journaling. I recall she was excited to go, but she was filled with nervousness. She shared with me that this was going to be her first flight in an airplane, her first time traveling internationally, and the first time in her life that she had been away from her twin sister and another sister who were both in her cohort but would not be attending. Prior to departure, she wondered if she could do it, but she not only survived, she thrived. One of the practices was to journal our daily experiences, allowing reflection on learnings and personal growth. Once introduced to journaling, she realized that she loved it. It allowed her to document her new adventures, and after a while, what was once a challenge became easy for her. Unlike other scholars, she couldn't just journal anywhere; some people initially thought she was isolating herself without a reason, but for her, journaling was a special time. Every night, she created a sanctuary, a space for her journaling to occur. Finding a quiet corner, Saidia would softly play music, grab her favorite pen, and begin to journal. The setting she created seemed transformative, a place where she could explore her thoughts, undisturbed. In the morning, she would change her scene, choosing the outdoors to sit on the porch, surrounded by nature's sounds or instrumental music. However, when the room was noisy, her perfect setting was disrupted, and her pen would barely touch the page. This observation spoke of the link between our environment and our ability to reflect. Her surroundings taught her that the environment matters.

Her journaling practice eventually became a ritual and a lesson for her peers once she explained her journaling method. She understood the essence of creating an environment that resonated with her, one that allowed her to reflect and journal. Reflecting on Saidia's sanctuary is a reminder to consider the environment for journaling. Ask yourself: What do you need to maximize your journaling experience? What will be your sanctuary?

Creating Your Space

- **Find a Quiet Place.** This could be your bedroom or a tranquil spot in a nearby park.
- **Comfort is Key.** Ensure your chosen space is comfortable.
- **Personalize Your Space.** Add elements that inspire tranquility and focus.
- **Consider Lighting.** Adjust the lighting to your preference.
- **Noise Control.** Whether you prefer soft background music or absolute silence, make sure your environment accommodates your needs.
- **Keep It Clean.** Maintain your space as tidy as possible. A clean space can help increase your ability to focus.

10 Essential Journaling Tips

1. **Commit to the process.** Try to develop consistency in terms of when you will journal.
2. **Don't edit. Just write.** There is no wrong answer.
3. **What's Right?** Write what feels right for you.
4. **Be honest.**
5. **Use the prompts.** Adapt them as needed.
6. **Experiment.** Explore different styles of journaling like single words, symbols, pictures, long and short narratives.

7. **Reflect and be descriptive**. What did you see, hear, feel, taste, touch, and experience? Describe the feeling as best you can in the way that allows you to express yourself.

8. **Be patient with yourself.**

9. **Date your entries.** Add the time if you like.

10. **Keep your journal private.**

JOURNAL
Take some time to Journal

_____

_____

_____

_____

_____

_____

_____

_____

_____

_____

_____

_____

_____

_____

_____

_____

_____

_____

_____

_____

_____

_____

_____

_____

_____

Dr. Katherine Y. Brown

The Importance of Why

A Guide to Purposeful Activities

Every child is born with an innate curiosity, a desire to understand the world around them. My four children, Anthony, Sydney, Irving, and Robert, were no exceptions. Each had their unique "But why?" that defined their childhood and taught me profound lessons about the desire for understanding.

Anthony was always the adventurous one. One day, while making a smoothie, he asked, "Why shouldn't you stick your hand in a blender?" I explained the dangers, emphasizing the sharpness of the blades. But a momentary lapse in my attention, and his curiosity got the better of him. The emergency room visit that followed was a reminder that sometimes, even explanations can't resolve the "But why?" that children harbor. Sometimes, words alone aren't enough.

Sydney was my naturalist. During our walks, she would enjoy looking at the chirping birds, the leaves, and listening to the sounds of nature. "Why does the river flow this way?" she would ask, or "Why does the wind whistle through the trees?" Each question was a window into her connection with nature and the world around her.

Irving, with his soulful disposition, had a soft spot for music. He would often hum along to tunes and rhythms, sometimes breaking into spontaneous dance. "Why does this beat make me want to move?" he'd ask.

I'd explain rhythm and melody, but Irving's "But why?" was more profound. It wasn't just about the music; it was about how the music made him feel.

Robert was my in-house engineer. He possessed a need to understand how things worked and loved calculating the distances of his paper airplanes based on different ways he made them. Clocks, toys, household gadgets–he'd dismantle them all to get to the heart of their mechanics. "But why does this gear turn that way?" he'd ask. Each disassembled toy was evidence of his goal to comprehend the intricacies of design and functionality.

As varied as their questions were, they all pointed towards a shared, human need: to understand, to dive deeper, to know the "why" behind everything. And as I've learned from Anthony, Sydney, Irving, and Robert, the journey of understanding is never-ending. Each activity, each exercise, invites you to look into the "why" and to nurture your curiosity. I hope you channel the inquisitiveness of your inner child, just like my children and discover the transformative power of "why."

Before jumping in, let's talk about the importance of understanding the "why" behind each activity:

1. Motivation Boost. Knowing why you're doing something can get you excited and keep you going. It's easier when you get the big picture.

2. Engaging with Purpose. When you know why an activity is good for you, you'll be more into it, getting all the good stuff out of it.

3. Measuring Effectiveness. Knowing the goals of each exercise helps you see if it's working for you. This way, you can pick what's best for you.

4. Relatability. Understanding the "why" makes sure the activities you pick match your personal dreams. It's about choosing things that feel right and help you the most.

5. Perseverance. When things get tough, remembering why you started can help you keep going. Don't give up. Keep looking for what works best for you.

6. Promotion of Deeper Learning. Instead of just doing what you're told, knowing the "why" helps you feel more connected to the material, making it work better for your well-being.

7. Advocacy. Sharing the good things about each activity can help spread happiness and help in your community.

"BUT WHY?" you might ask. I'm so glad you're wondering!

Including the "why" in this book is on purpose. I want to help you make good decisions about your mental health journey. This book is more than just a list of things to do; it's full of helpful tools, each with a special purpose. As you read through the pages, always think about the "why" and let it help you make the most of this book.

Reflections
Why I Journal

I've been reminded of countless conversations I'd had throughout my career. Time and again, professionals shared with me their feelings of constant stress and exhaustion. It wasn't just professionals either. Students opened up about their struggles, and many shared a similar remedy: journaling.

It made sense. When times had gotten tough for them, writing their thoughts gave them a sense of relief. But there was a challenge. Many felt stuck, unsure of what to write. I remembered the strategies I used back in my 20s, working as an occupational therapist in what were then called psychiatric units and/or behavioral health units for both adults and adolescents. There were so many tools and insights I'd picked up. That's when a light bulb went off in my head. Why not provide journal prompts, affirmations, and helpful tips?

But I wanted more perspectives. That's why, in the next chapter, you'll hear from individuals who've made journaling a part of their lives. They've found growth, comfort, and positive outcomes from this practice. While their stories don't cover every reason or method of journaling, they showcase its many benefits.

I genuinely hope their experiences inspire you. Once you start journaling, you'll discover its transformative power. You've got this, and the journey ahead is full of promise.

A Conversation with Robert D. Brown

Hi, I'm Robert D. Brown, currently in my sophomore year at Father Ryan High School in Nashville, Tennessee. I'm the youngest of four siblings: Anthony, age 30; Sydney, age 23; and Irving, age 22. Being the youngest by a wide margin, I've often felt a push to carve out my own path and find my unique interests. My freshman year at Father Ryan High School truly reflected that spirit of exploration and determination. I participated in various activities, joining the cross country, swimming, and tennis teams. I also participated in the cooking club, multicultural club, and chamber choir. On top of that, I was proud to make both the academic dean's list and receive the principal's award.

Now, you might think that's just high school stuff but for me, it was a big shift from my middle school years. Back in 7th grade, I faced bullying, which led to an urgent transfer by my mom to a different public school. Then in 8th grade, I transitioned to an academic magnet middle school. Shuffling through three schools in just two years was hard. During this time, my mom recommended writing as an outlet. Although many boys I knew didn't really talk about journaling, I tried it. This became a tool for me, helping me articulate my feelings, set my sights on my goals, and make sense of my world.

2020 brought a challenge none of us expected–the COVID-19 pandemic. Like most students, I was abruptly shifted to virtual learning, isolated from the familiarity of classmates and school routines. This sudden change weighed heavily on many, including me. Conversations around feeling alone, distanced, and frustrated became common.

Fast forward to 2023, and the impact of COVID-19 is still evident. There's a growing conversation around mental health, emphasizing the need for support and understanding. While social media presents both pros and cons, it cannot replicate the warmth and connection we get from face-to-face interactions with friends and family. The reflections in this book come from individuals opening up about their mental health journeys. Through their stories, they want to remind you that your mental well-being is essential. Everyone has their own coping mechanisms, and for me, it includes exercise, swimming, tennis, jogging and journaling.

If you ever find yourself overwhelmed, remember it's completely okay to seek help, whether from a trusted individual, a medical professional, or any other reliable source. Journaling and positive affirmations have been game-changers for me and many of my friends. And one key takeaway? You're never alone in your struggles. This book symbolizes the strength in community. I encourage you to explore journaling–find prompts that resonate with you and make reflection a regular habit. Always remember, you matter, and so does your mental health and well-being.

Journey:
A Conversation with Zeboreh Bynum and Trenay Perry Bynum

Everyone has special places or activities that make them feel good and calm inside. Think of "happy places" or safe spots where our minds can take a break and relax. These places can be anywhere—maybe a cozy corner in your room, a park you love to visit, or even a hobby you enjoy. Recognizing and spending time in these "happy places" can be like giving yourself a mini-vacation. When life gets busy, tricky, or overwhelming it's essential to know where our happy place is, so we have somewhere to go, even if just in our thoughts, to feel better. In essence, we each need a happy place and finding it is part of our journey. As we think about the acronym J.O.U.R.N.A.L., I wanted to highlight the voice of people who can share reflections into a glimpse of their journey. I hope that their stories resonate with you in some way in the hope that you will begin to journal on your journey to finding a place that protects your mental health and happiness.

Hello, I am KYB Leader Zeboreh Bynum. I am a member of KYB Cohort: 16. I attend Hume Fogg High School and am a junior.

Why is finding a happy place essential for mental health?

I have learned that life is a series of decisions. Each choice we make results in something we either like or don't like. When we experience life, we experience feelings. I remember the example of a soda pop can that was shaken. The can gets full of fizz, and the soda splatters like a volcano when you open it. Our feelings are like that. When we get shaken up too much and we don't deal with our feelings we may pop–splatter our negative emotions everywhere.

We need to find a happy place when our feelings get out of control. This does not mean a vacation or leaving where we are, it just means finding a place where we can feel better and take good care of our mental health. Each day gives us a chance to appreciate something good in life and discover a happy place. When you find a happy place among the chaos of life you learn to protect your mental health.

My happy place is on the floor doing art. My other happy place is in the kitchen baking something sweet. I absolutely love doing art and cooking! It's like my secret world where I can express myself in the most colorful and delicious ways. I've been drawing and painting for as long as I can remember. The feeling of a blank piece of paper, book cover, or a crisp white paper is just magical. When I put my brush to the paper, it's like the colors come alive, and I can create anything I dream up. Sometimes, I get lost in my own world of colors and shapes, and hours fly by without me even noticing.

Cooking, on the other hand, is like a tasty adventure. I remember the first time I made marshmallows from scratch, and the kitchen was filled with the sweet scent of freshly baked treats. My family's faces lit up with joy when they tasted my marshmallows–my mother used them in her coffee!

I feel like I can create anything in my happy place, which is often right at the kitchen counter or with my art supplies spread out. Sometimes my creations don't come out all that great but I keep trying. Whether it's experimenting with new recipes or trying out different art techniques, there's always something new to learn and discover.

I may be just 16 years old, but I already know that art and cooking will always be a part of my life. They're my happy places, my creative outlets, and my ways of bringing joy to the people I care about. Who knows what amazing masterpieces and culinary delights I'll create in the future?

I draw faces to show if my family liked the food I baked. These notes to myself have been fun to read especially when I read my notes from the time I was much younger. Our happy place doesn't have to be a place we go to. Our happy place can be right where we are, doing what we love to do.

Chiming in.

"Zeboreh will speak fire out of her mouth!" These were the words shared with me from Mamma Brenda, a member of my church. Zeboreh was not even a year and Mamma Brenda was given a word from God that Zeboreh will develop a powerful voice. Here's what is so interesting. We taught Zeboreh sign language as an infant so there doesn't seem to be a time in her life that she couldn't communicate. We've always looked for ways to allow Zeboreh to develop her voice and be fearless in using it. We still have mixed feelings about the _fearlessness._

Zeboreh's voice was stifled after she left kindergarten. In first grade, she was made to sit quietly in her Montessori environment. She was admonished several times for speaking too much. Finding the right educational environment for her was difficult in our family. My husband and I sided with the teachers, believing the adults were always right. We aided in stifling Zeboreh's voice. After a really difficult time in two private schools, we enrolled Zeboreh in the neighborhood school. The fourth grade teacher invited me for a meeting four weeks into the school year. I immediately thought that Zeboreh was in trouble. The teacher asked me to recount the trouble other teachers experienced and after my retelling about Zeboreh speaking up too much, hiding under the desk to read books, and being too playful, the teacher said, "That's what fourth graders do!" Silent tears rolled down my face.

My vivacious child was not a problem nor was her voice. Unfortunately, she began hiding things – her liquid concoctions of soap and water, her cookies, and her voice. Then, there was a breakthrough. I'm skipping through this story a bit, but two things showed us that Zeboreh Hannah (From the Creator, God's Gift) would not be squashed.

The first was in middle school. Her first day of school, I received a panicked call from a teacher. I could hear Zeboreh yelling in the background. She calmed down by the time I arrived at the school's office but I'll never forget what she said. "I will not be mistreated! I dealt with this at [school shall remain nameless to protect the innocent–humph!]. I will not deal with this here!" I was floored and trying to figure out if I should also be embarrassed. But, the women at John Early Museum Magnet Middle School put their arms around my child and consoled her while explaining that they were there to protect her and she was loved. Finally, teachers saw her and allowed her to be who God created her to be. My child is going to be fine.

The last example was while on an educational trip with the Dr. Katherine Y. Brown Leadership Academy (KYB). Zeboreh was selected for the travel team to teach leadership principles to students on Turks and Caicos. One of our excursions was on a boat for sightseeing. We came upon a huge ship that was rusted and stuck in the middle of an ocean. The students–secured in life-jackets–jumped in the water and headed for the ship. Zeboreh pleaded with Dad and me to allow her to do it. I could only really think about all the bad that could happen. Dad said let her do it and off she went. By the time she climbed to the top of the ship, doubt set in and she was too afraid to jump off. We called out encouragement. Others jumped off to show her how easy it was. After what seemed like an hour, she held her nose and jumped! She dealt with her fear and jumped. My child is going to be fine.

When we hear the word journal we may just think about recording the news and events in our life. Another definition is a record of experiences, ideas, or reflections kept regularly.

In the journey of Zeboreh's life, we've witnessed the profound transformation of her voice, from the prophetic words of Mamma Brenda to her fearless spirit in childhood. It's a story of trials and triumphs, of moments when her vibrant voice was stifled, but also of moments when she defied expectations.

Zeboreh's courage shone through school misadventures, where she refused mistreatment and found a supportive community that embraced her uniqueness. The pivotal moment on that boat, facing her fear and taking the leap, encapsulates her resilience and determination.

Her journey reminds us that a journal isn't just a record of events; it's a chronicle of growth, self-discovery, and the unwavering spirit within. Our journals accompany us on our journey through life. Zeboreh Hannah has emerged from these experiences stronger than ever, and we have no doubt that her voice will continue to inspire and empower others. She is indeed going to be more than fine.

Optimism:
A Conversation with Lillian Floyd-Thomas

I'm Lillian, a 9th grader from Harpeth Hall High School, part of KYB Leadership Academy Cohort 29. I aspire to become an author and screenwriter.

Optimism is your chosen word. What does it mean to you?

Optimism to me means to not let small inconveniences ruin your perspective or make you give up. I believe optimism goes hand in hand with perseverance. When you're optimistic and persevering you don't let what is wrong determine your outcome but keep on pushing for something better.

How do you define mental health?

Mental health to me means not putting too much pressure on yourself and realizing how everything you do impacts you and your mind. It means being flexible but also knowing what's best for you, and what your limits are so that you don't overuse yourself and you are able to be the best you possible.

Why is it important to journal?

It's important to journal because it's another way to express your thoughts and emotions when it might be hard at times. Sometimes you might not want to say something in case you hurt someone's feelings, or you need to think out how you feel. It's not good to keep your feelings bottled up, and journaling your feelings is a way to release all your feelings and think about your actions before you act.

What is your favorite way to relax?

I enjoy reading or listening to music when I want to relax.

Have you learned any unexpected lessons related to optimism and mental health?

I learned the key to mental health is to realize that if your life matters to you, you must keep your "mind over matter." This cliche is a valuable life lesson because our ability to use our minds to govern our perspective in the moment when situations or problems seem out of our control can be the key to optimism in the face of obstacles.

What are your dreams for the future of mental health?

For the future of mental health I hope to see maybe more classes or electives in schools that actually have projects that students do instead of just watching videos or telling kids to just get off their phones. Maybe instead use phones as a way to reach people who struggle with mental health, and create an app that gives people activities to do and tracks people's growth in their mental health. Maybe an app like Tik Tok but it's specifically meant for mental health videos and activities.

Lastly, can you share some journaling prompts that help maintain optimism?

1. What are exercises that you use to stay positive?
2. What are ways to spread positivity?
3. Do you believe that you are optimistic/ positive?
4. What has been your journey to get to positivity/ how do you plan to become more positive?
5. Create a morning mantra for yourself to start the day right and to remind yourself to stay positive.
6. Write about a situation that wasn't going well, but got better because of your mindset.
7. Who is the most positive person you know, and how do you feel when you are around them?
8. What is your favorite thing about yourself?
9. Try to say only positive things got a day and explain how it made you feel and how others reacted.
10. What would you do if your best friend needed to be cheered up?

Are there any words of wisdom you would share with others?

My words of wisdom are from a poem I heard in the movie Akeelah and the Bee. It's called Our Deepest Fear by Marianne Williamson.

Understanding:
A Conversation with Cydney Elliott

I am Cydney Elliott a sophomore student at Tennessee State University. I am a member of cohort 7 of KYB Leadership Academy. I aspire to work in the field of law.

You mentioned your involvement with the Dr. Katherine Y. Brown (KYB) Leadership Academy. Could you elaborate on that?

Being part of the KYB Leadership Academy has been an enriching experience. I was recognized as the KYB Leader of the Year and served as an Alumni Ambassador. The academy has provided me with numerous opportunities. I traveled to Beatrice, Alabama to raise awareness of pulmonary hypertension and talk about leadership as part of the KYB Leadership Academy Conference held there. I've also had international experiences, attending the KYB Leadership Academy International Conferences, specifically traveling to Dubai in 2018, Costa Rica in 2019, and Turks and Caicos in 2021.

Your chosen topic is 'Understanding.' Why is that significant for you?

Understanding mental health is needed for the strength and unity of our communities. Things like depression and anxiety have a major impact. But to support each other, we need to stop misconceptions about mental health.

This seems deeply personal to you.

Yes, my perspective comes from personal experience. I've been diagnosed with ADHD, anxiety, and depression. Initially, these challenges made my academic and personal life hard, but I got help. Through therapy and self-awareness, I've learned not just to cope but to thrive.

How do you manage your mental health?

Journaling has been instrumental for me. Documenting my fears, thoughts, and feelings has given me clarity. I also find coloring, especially in a park, a way to de-stress and focus.

Any lessons you've learned along the way?

One essential takeaway is the power of sharing struggles. It can lead to the support one needs. Therapy can be a challenge that turns into a learning opportunity.

What's your vision for the future of mental health?

I dream of a world where mental health discussions are mainstream. I envision easy access to resources for everyone, devoid of any attached stigma.

Could you share some journal prompts that help with understanding mental health?

1. Describe a mental health challenge you've faced.
2. Reflect on your mental health journey's evolution.
3. Think of someone who supported your mental health journey.
4. What are your self-care practices?
5. Write about helping someone with their mental health.
6. Draft a letter to your future self.
7. Discuss a misconception you once held about mental health.
8. Detail a time you successfully managed stress.
9. If there was no judgment, what would you share about your mental health journey?
10. How has your journey shaped your life perspective?

Do you have any concluding thoughts for our readers?

Every one of us faces challenges. But with understanding and self-care, we can navigate these obstacles. Treasure your journey and remember that each step represents progress and personal growth.

JOURNAL
Take some time to Journal

_____

_____

_____

_____

_____

_____

_____

_____

_____

_____

_____

_____

_____

_____

_____

_____

_____

_____

_____

_____

_____

_____

_____

_____

_____

_____

Reflection:
A Conversation with TiNiah Abernathy

I'm TiNiah Abernathy, a junior at Tennessee State University (TSU). I'm currently majoring in Nursing with aspirations to become a pediatric nursing practitioner. Additionally, I'm proud to serve as the president of Cohort 26 of the Dr. Katherine Y. Brown Leadership Academy at TSU.

Reflection seems to be a pivotal theme in your life. Could you expand on its significance?
From a young age, my mother emphasized the value of reflection. She believed in grounding oneself, analyzing past decisions, and understanding the emotions accompanying those choices. Although initially daunting, reflection has been instrumental in my growth. It's helped me discover my joys, plan for the future, cultivate relationships, and hone my leadership abilities.

Mental health is another theme closely tied to reflection. How would you describe its importance?
Mental health is comprehensive, influencing us socially, physiologically, emotionally, and cognitively. It's not just a concern for a select few with diagnoses but a crucial aspect of everyone's well-being. Good mental health isn't just the absence of illness but the capability to handle life's stresses and remain productive.

You've mentioned journaling as a medium of reflection. Can you share your personal experience?

I've recently started journaling, and it's been transformative for my emotional health. The act of journaling helps decompress, process emotions, and organize thoughts. I've kept both electronic and paper journals, and revisiting them has been insightful. During my nursing program's inception last spring semester, I journaled weekly and even blogged about my journey. This practice showcased my growth and reinforced my appreciation for the path I believe God has set for me.

What advice would you offer our readers regarding reflection?

I'd invite everyone to embrace reflection. Whether it's through journaling, spending quiet moments, enjoying nature, or just dedicated alone time–prioritize it. Mental well-being is paramount. We must move it up our priority list and give it the attention it merits.

Could you share some journal prompts for those interested in starting the practice?

1. What were your expectations for today?
2. Did you feel equipped for the day?
3. How do you boost yourself when venturing into something new?
4. What do you cherish about your personality?
5. What challenges have you overcome recently?
6. What would you pursue if failure wasn't an option?
7. How have you evolved this year?
8. What brought you joy this week?
9. What often frustrates you?
10. For what are you most thankful?

Do you have any final thoughts or wisdom to share with our readers?

I often recite Proverbs 3:5: "Trust in the Lord with all your heart, lean not unto your own understanding but in everything acknowledge the Lord and he will direct your path." This scripture is a gift from my mother, who believes Proverbs offer life's wisdom. It reminds me that God is always in control. Find solace and reassurance in Him; He's always with us.

Nurturing:
A Conversation with Amara L. King

Hi there! My name is Amara L. King. I'm a proud member of Cohort 29 and currently studying at Brentwood High School. I just transitioned from 9th to 10th grade–how time flies! Career-wise, I'm leaning towards the music and art industry or possibly entrepreneurship and law.

What topic have you chosen for your input in the J.O.U.R.N.A.L.?

I've selected the theme of Nurturing. To me, nurturing revolves around caring for and encouraging the growth or development of oneself and others. It's about being aware of personal experiences and learning how to bounce back. It's crucial to recognize the weight of words–they might not break bones, but they can chip away at one's spirit.

Mental health seems to be a significant theme in your narrative. Can you tell us more about its importance to you?

Mental well-being is of paramount importance to me. Physical injuries might heal over time, but scars on the soul take longer. We all want to remember our past fondly, so it's vital to prioritize mental health. When the days get tough, turning to prayer and journaling can provide solace.

How do you personally deal with challenging days?

I've got a few go-to remedies. Listening to music, reading, diving into a favorite show, playing with a pet, praying, napping, or even just a good cry. All these activities help lower my stress and offer an escape from the present moment.

You shared that you had thoughts regarding therapy, can you share them?

Even though I haven't attended a session, I'm all for it! Therapy can be a positive step for mental health, offering a platform to share struggles. It's never too late to seek help.

What unexpected lesson have you derived from your experiences?

It's crucial to slow down and self-reflect. We often move so fast that we don't recognize the toll certain situations take on us. Pausing and self-checking can be enlightening.

What future do you envision for mental health awareness?

I hope to see signs of mental health emphasis everywhere–schools, offices, homes, religious institutions, camps, and so on. Mental well-being should intertwine with daily life. It's a dream I genuinely hope becomes a norm.

Do you have a personal mantra for tough times?

I always remind myself, "I am stronger than what lies ahead." No matter how bleak the present may seem, I believe God never burdens us beyond our capacity. Self-belief is incredibly empowering.

Could you provide some journal prompts for our readers?

1. Do I feel worthy of nurturing and care?
2. How can I treat myself better this year?
3. What are 5 actions for self-nurturing and self-care?
4. What's currently occupying unnecessary mental space?
5. What heightens my stress and how can I alleviate it?
6. Would I like to read more this year? Which book?
7. List 10 incredible things my body accomplishes.
8. How can I improve my sleep quality this year?
9. Who can I contact for love and support?
10. How is my spirit? How can I foster a closer bond with God?

Do you have any final words for our readers?

Always remember: "You are more precious than jewels."
- Proverbs 31:10.

JOURNAL
Take some time to Journal

Acceptance:
A Conversation with Alivia Kallie Dove

Hello! I'm Alivia Kallie Dove, a senior at Father Ryan High School and part of KYB Leadership Academy Cohort 29. My career aspiration is to become a nurse anesthetist.

The term you've chosen is Acceptance. Why is it meaningful to you?

To me, acceptance is about understanding and loving something or someone for who they truly are. It has been a key element in my journey with mental health. Often, life brings us situations that, for our peace of mind, we simply have to accept.

How do you view mental health?

Mental health, for me, is an act of loving oneself. It's essential because if we don't love and accept ourselves, it becomes challenging to offer the same love and acceptance to others.

What role does journaling play in your life?

Journaling is invaluable for mental well-being as it provides an outlet, especially when therapy isn't an option. Writing offers a way to express both positive and negative emotions freely.

Do you have any relaxation methods?

Yes, I find solace in listening to calming folk music and diving into a good book.

Any lessons or aspirations you'd like to share?

One lesson that stands out is realizing that sometimes life's distractions or obstacles are just deviations from God's true path for us. As for the future, I hope to build healthier relationships with some people.

Lastly, do you have a personal mantra or message you'd like to impart?

"Be the reason someone feels welcomed, seen, heard, valued, loved, and supported." This mantra keeps me grounded. Kindness requires so little effort, and I always aim to positively impact the lives of others.

You've provided some journal prompts on the theme of acceptance. Can you share them with us?

1. Why is acceptance important?
2. What are some areas you struggle with when it comes to acceptance?
3. Why is acceptance challenging for you?
4. How can you come to terms with things that don't always go your way?
5. At what age did acceptance start to matter to you and why?

6. Where did you hear the term acceptance?

7. Can acceptance be tied to other situations and people?

8. What relationships have affected your perspective on acceptance?

9. Do you believe society talks enough about the importance of accepting differences? Discuss ways that it's working well or ways that it can be improved.

10. In your daily interactions, do you find it easier to accept people as they are or do you wish for them to change to your expectations?

LOVE:
A Conversation with Lauryn Smith

I'm Lauryn Smith, currently a freshman at Davidson Academy. I'm part of the KYB Leadership Academy Cohort 29 and I aspire to be a pediatrician.

The word you've chosen to discuss today is "Love." What does it signify for you?

To me, love means having a deep feeling of intense affection. It's characterized by emotions and behaviors that encompass intimacy, passion, and commitment. Through my mental health journey, I've learned the depth of self-love and care.

How would you define mental health from your perspective?

Mental health is about being in a state where you can cope with life's stresses. It's essential because it shapes our thoughts, emotions, and actions. It's the anchor that helps us manage stress, bond with others, and make informed, healthy decisions.

Journaling is a prevalent self-care method. Why do you feel it's crucial for mental health?

Journaling has been a revelation for many, including myself. It's a space where you can express feelings, perhaps more clearly than when speaking.

How do you like to unwind and relax?

I'm drawn to the arts, so I enjoy activities like drawing and painting. Additionally, spending time with my friends is always refreshing.

Are there any unexpected lessons you've learned along your journey?

One thing I've come to realize is the importance of moving forward and trusting that God is always there to guide and support.

Do you have a specific vision or hope for your mental well-being in the future?

I hope to gain more control over my emotions. It's about finding a balance and maintaining it.

Is there a mantra or saying you live by?

I often remind myself of a quote I once heard: "Therefore do not worry about tomorrow, for tomorrow will worry about itself. Each day has enough trouble of its own."

Before we wrap up, would you mind sharing some journal prompts related to Love?

1. Write about a time you looked in the mirror and truly appreciated something about yourself.
2. Describe your favorite memory and what makes it so special.
3. Plan and describe your ideal pampering routine for a day of self-care.
4. Find a quote about self-love. Write it down and reflect on what it means to you.
5. Describe three traits you genuinely love about yourself and why.
6. List and reflect on 10 aspects of your body that you're grateful for or love.
7. Which part of your life are you currently most content with? Elaborate.
8. Discuss a recent achievement or moment you were genuinely proud of.
9. Reflect on 4 physical features you love about yourself and why.
10. Think about feedback from family members. What is something they often say they love or appreciate about you?

JOURNAL
Take some time to Journal

_____

_____

_____

_____

_____

_____

_____

_____

_____

_____

_____

_____

_____

_____

_____

_____

_____

_____

_____

_____

_____

_____

_____

_____

_____

_____

_____

_____

_____

JOURNAL

A Conversation with Hallie Sheffield

I'm Hallie Sheffield. I attend Hendersonville High School. I am a senior. I am a member of KYB Leadership Academy Cohort 29.

What are your career aspirations?

My career aspiration is agriculture and marketing.

Which word have you chosen to represent a key concept in your life, and what does it mean to you?

My chosen word is 'Acceptance.' Acceptance to me means to have love and respect for someone no matter the flaws, struggles, or troubles they have. It means acknowledging someone as they are without judgment or the desire to change them.

How would you define mental health?

In my mind, mental health means putting your well-being and state of mind in the healthiest condition possible. It's about having good coping mechanisms to help you deal with issues that can be challenging.

Why do you find journaling important?

To me, journaling can be another way to express feelings in a healthy way. Keeping in emotions for too long could make you feel worse. It can be an emotional

71

outlet or stress reducer that can help you cope with stressful experiences in life.

What's your favorite way to relax and unwind?

My favorite way to relax is to go outside and be with close friends and family. I enjoy traveling and exploring new places throughout.

Could you share an unexpected lesson you've learned in your life?

My biggest, unexpected lesson would be that people can seem friendly but turn out only to pretend to be friends with you. This can be very disappointing and cause emotional damages like trust issues.

Where do you envision yourself in the future?

My dream for the future is to be in the food science field. I would like to pursue a career as a quality assurance director with the USDA that helps oversee the scientific study and understanding of the production, processing, preservation, and distribution of food in our country.

Do you have a personal mantra or philosophy that guides your life?

Comparing myself to others will not feed me. Collaboration and community involvement will fulfill me. I will inspire others, and I will allow others to inspire me.

Can you elaborate on what acceptance means to you on a personal level?

I want to share an excerpt of a journal I wrote today that is about what acceptance means to me.

I realized that every step I take is just part of a bigger path of self-acceptance. It's also about understanding that, even when things get rough, my feelings and experiences are totally valid. It isn't a one-time thing, it's a continuous process. I'm reminded that I am on a path of growth and every step I take helps with my journey of self-acceptance. It's about realizing that my emotions and experiences are valid, even when they seem difficult. I will start acknowledging my strengths and flaws without judging myself and choosing to move forward.

Thank you for sharing that. Have you had any experiences that made you feel not accepted, isolated or excluded?

I recall a time when I was at a sleepover activity. I often found myself in a situation where the other kids would form their own close-knit groups, leaving me feeling isolated and disconnected. It was a challenging experience as I genuinely wanted to be a part of their conversations and activities. I tried to join in, to be a part of their jokes and stories, but too often, it seemed as if I were invisible. Was it because I'm not naturally loud or assertive? I couldn't help but wonder why this seemed to happen to me repeatedly. This question left me deeply frustrated to the point where I sometimes stopped trying altogether. I would withdraw into my quiet self, thinking that maybe if I stayed in the background, I wouldn't face rejection. This approach didn't help either. It left me feeling even more disconnected and, at times, doubting my self-worth. When the activity ended, all I wanted to do is be in a safe environment where I could be myself without judgment.

What did this experience teach you about inclusion and acceptance?

This experience made me realize the importance of reaching out to those who may be feeling isolated within a group. A simple act of inclusion can have a huge impact on their experience and make them feel a sense of belonging. If only those who are doing the isolation understand the impact their actions are having on others maybe, they would change how they interact. It also reinforced the idea that acceptance extends beyond ourselves, it's about creating an inclusive and supportive environment for others as well.

How has someone else's story influenced your perspective on acceptance?

Thinking back to Cydney Elliott's story, I'm reminded of her journey of acceptance. Her candid account of battling anxiety, depression, and ADHD resonates deeply with me. Her words remind me that I'm not alone in my struggles. I draw inspiration from her willingness to share her experiences, embracing vulnerability as a pathway to connection and understanding. This is why I choose to share my experiences.

Can you share an instance where you supported someone else in their journey towards acceptance?

I recall a time when I helped a friend on their mental health journey. It reminded me that acceptance isn't solely an inward journey; it's also about acceptance and support for others. I remember my friend who confided in me about her battles of depression and some days she didn't want to get out of bed to go to school. And sometimes at school others wouldn't get some of her quirks and qualities. She said that it seemed like everyone around her was striving to fit into a certain mold of what they thought was "popular or normal". But we both agreed that everyone should just be themselves. As we both talked and became better friends, we both realized that you must just learn how to accept yourself.

To conclude, can you offer some reflections on your journey of acceptance?

Yes. I believe that it's possible to overcome these feelings of not being accepted. The journey towards self-acceptance and finding acceptance from others can take time and effort, but it's achievable. It often involves ongoing self-reflection and growth and support from friends and family. Everyone's path is unique, and progress may come in stages, but I have determination that it will come.

JOURNAL
Take some time to Journal

Lessons Learned From A Block Party

Growing up on the Southside of Chicago, Illinois, at 117th and Halsted, I have memories that will stay with me forever. Our summer block parties weren't just events; they were lessons in unity, resilience, and mental well-being.

What's a block party? It's a big get-together on our street, with everyone from the block joining in. We'd set up tables with food, chairs, and games. The aroma of barbecue would pull neighbors out of their homes and into the shared fun.

Kids ran around, laughing and playing. Sometimes, someone would open up a fire hydrant, and we'd all dash into the cooling spray. Music kept everyone's energy high, with tunes for every generation. Dancing, singing, just being in the moment–it was pure joy.

For the adults, it wasn't just about relaxation. They'd talk, share stories, and give support. Bringing just one dish of food meant you could enjoy everything else that others had brought to offer. It was all about sharing and caring.

But there was more to these parties than met the eye. They were our community's way of taking care of our mental health. Being together, sharing laughs and stories, and dancing stress away–it was therapy without a formal name. We leaned on each other, celebrated each other, and lifted each other up.

Drawing from those memories, I see the power of community in supporting mental health. Imagine if we took the essence of those block parties and infused them into regular journaling get-togethers. Groups coming together to express to read this book that is in your hands, share ideas, and heal through writing. Sharing stories, offering words of encouragement, and creating a safe space to let out feelings. This would not only build strong bonds but would be a step toward ensuring that everyone has a support system.

The mental health benefits of journaling are well-known. It's a form of self-reflection and an outlet for emotions. Combining journaling with community gatherings, just like our block parties, could be transformative. The feeling of not being alone in one's struggles, the support from peers, and the act of writing for self-care can lead to profound healing.

In essence, our block parties taught me the value of community. Similarly, journaling, when practiced collectively, can be a powerful tool that binds a community. Taking it a step further I want to suggest that you consider community journaling parties could be a powerful tool for mental well-being, showing that together, we can always find strength, support, and healing.

Making sure that everyone has a personal copy of this book is vital as it serves as a guide for this communal journey. The stories, quotes, and insights within are meant to be returned to and shared repeatedly. Each chapter of this book holds value not just for individual reflection, but for group discussions and shared enlightenment.

Reflecting on our journey is essential, but doing so in a supportive community can amplify its impact. By understanding and empathizing with others stories and experiences, we enrich our own. This mirrors the essence of those block parties from my childhood where every individual, by merely participating, added value to the collective celebration. I encourage you to reflect independently and also when the opportunity presents itself to be around others for a community journaling circle. This allows you to share your reflections, engage with others, and truly embrace the power of community journaling. It's in these shared experiences that the lessons from our individual journeys have a unique opportunity to gain broader meaning.

Here's an example:

KYB Leadership Academy Team Building Activity: "Community Journaling Circle"

Objective:
To foster unity, promote shared reflection, and enhance mental well-being through community journaling.

Materials Needed:

- A copy of this book for each participant.
- Journals or notepads.
- Pens or pencils.
- A comfortable space to sit, either chairs in a circle or cushions on the floor.
- Soft background music (optional).

Instructions for the Community Journaling Circle:

Setting the Tone: Begin by creating a warm and welcoming atmosphere. Ensure everyone is seated comfortably, with their copy of **this** book, a journal or notepad, and a pen or pencil. If you choose to have music, play it softly in the background to foster a relaxed mood.

Introductions: If participants don't know each other, or even if they do, take a few minutes for everyone to introduce themselves. Sharing a favorite quote or a particular chapter from this book can be a good icebreaker.

Guided Reading: Select a passage or a quote from this book. Read it aloud to the group, and then allow a few moments of silence for everyone to reflect on it personally.

Writing Prompt: Following the reading, provide a journaling prompt related to the passage or quote. For example, after reading a quote about understanding, the prompt could be, "Write about a time you felt truly understood by others and how it impacted your mental well-being."

Sharing and Discussion: After everyone has had some time to write, invite participants to share what they've written. This is voluntary; no one should feel pressured to share. Encourage active listening, with participants responding empathetically and without judgment.

Group Reflection: Conclude the journaling circle by having a group reflection. Discuss the themes or common threads that arose during the session. This can be a time to offer words of encouragement, share insights, and celebrate the power of community.

Closing: Thank everyone for their contributions and participation. Express hope that they'll continue these practices, both independently and within the community, to further foster mental well-being.

Final Thoughts: Block Party Memories of Unity and Healing

As the sun would set on our block parties, the music fading into a gentle hum, and the streets returning to their usual calm, the essence of the day remained. It wasn't just about the barbecue, the dancing, or the shared laughter; it was about the unity we forged and the memories we created.

The block parties of my childhood were more than events. They were moments of collective resilience, times when a community came together not only to celebrate but also to support and uplift. As we wrap up this chapter, I want to impress upon you the idea that those parties weren't isolated moments of joy, but symbolic representations of the community's spirit–a spirit that remains relevant and needed today.

In our fast-paced world, it's easy to get lost in the hustle, to forget the value of pausing, reflecting, and, most importantly, connecting. Just like those block parties, a community journaling circle isn't solely about writing on paper. It's about writing on the soul–it's about understanding oneself and understanding others, realizing that while our journeys might differ, the emotions, challenges, and victories often resonate similarly.

I invite you to carry the spirit of the block parties with you, not just in memories but in action. Embrace the power of community, whether it's in journaling circles, group discussions, or simply moments where you pause and listen, really listen, to those around you.

Your story, the challenges you've overcome, the milestones you've celebrated, and the dreams you hold for the future are pieces of your life. When we explore our stories together, when we share, reflect, and support as a community, it becomes a testament to human spirit and resilience. Remember, every block party might end, but its lessons and the unity it fosters can last a lifetime. Embrace your journey, share it, and let it be a source of hope and inspiration for others.

JOURNAL
Take some time to Journal

Pedals, Falls, and Affirmations:

Navigating Life's Journey

With the Dr. Katherine Y. Brown (KYB) Leadership Academy, I never pass up an opportunity to remind our scholars about the powerful trinity of words, thoughts, and actions. These lessons are particularly important to me, as I learned their significance after many missteps and stumbles–literally.

My comically vivid memory is of my attempts to ride a bike. Picture it: a tall child (that's me) eyeing a bright orange and yellow bike. This wasn't just any bike, though. It sported a flashy banana seat that screamed for attention. But what stood out even more? The two, very noticeable, training wheels. I wasn't that happy about the training wheels, but the bike was impressive. I don't remember my exact age but I was probably about ten years old.

I was motivated by a goal–I want to ride a bike–but my inner voice was focused on something different. "What if I fall?" And in the noisy parking lot with laughing kids all around, those words became reality. My first attempt was an epic fail. Down I went! But as the laughter intensified, my mother's voice resonated through: "What others say doesn't define you. It's your words, your thoughts, and your actions that truly matter."

She was right. My self-talk and thoughts needed a change. Replacing my "I might fall" with "If I fall, I'll get back up," I began my wobbly journey once again for what seemed like a daily trial and error over several months. Imagine watching a toddler trying to walk for the first time. Now scale that up to my size. That's right! It was a comical sight–a tall child, long legs flailing, trying to balance on a bike meant for much younger riders. But with each topple and rise, and with words of encouragement from my biggest cheerleader, my mom, I eventually ditched those training wheels. My hilarious struggle turned into a triumphant ride.

This ordeal wasn't just about riding a bike. It introduced me to the powerful force of affirmations. I had to change my mindset before I could master the physical task of riding a bike.

Affirmations: The Power to Steer Our Journey

Life can sometimes feel like learning to ride a bike. At times, you might feel unsteady, unsure, and even scared. There might be days when you feel like giving up, where every pedal seems harder than the last. But just as with riding a bike, it's in these challenging moments that we truly grow.

I've learned that the words we tell ourselves during these times can either propel us forward or keep us stuck in a rut. Affirmations are those words; they're the encouraging whispers we need to hear, especially during the hardest parts of our journey.

Drawing from the ups and downs of learning to ride that orange and yellow bike with its long banana seat, I've crafted some affirmations for you. Let them be your guide, your gentle push forward when you need it most.

Bike-inspired Affirmations

- If I fall, I'll get back up.
- Every day, I'm learning to find my balance.
- I might wobble, but I'm still moving forward.
- Every pedal forward is a step towards my goals.
- It's okay to have training wheels; we all need support sometimes.
- No one gets it right the first time.
- Every journey starts with having the courage to start; today, I will begin.
- I'll keep pedaling, even when the road gets tough.
- I'm alive and making progress.
- Each ride, no matter how short or long, is a victory to celebrate.
- Just like riding a bike, life is about balance and momentum.

Each affirmation, just like every pedal on a bike, can propel you forward. Whenever you're faced with self-doubt or challenges on your journey towards better mental health, turn to these affirmations. Speak them out loud, write them down, or simply reflect on them. They are designed to be your compass, pointing you in the direction of resilience, growth, and perseverance. Celebrate every victory, no matter its size, and remember that the journey itself is just as valuable as the destination.

JOURNAL
Take some time to Journal

101 Ways To Unlocking Your Thoughts:
The Healing Power of Journal Prompts

Journaling is more than just a practice of writing–it's a pathway to mental wellness. By translating our thoughts to words on paper, you have an opportunity to create a safe space for self-expression, reflection, and healing. However, finding the right words or even knowing where to start can be challenging. This is where journal prompts step in.

Imagine these prompts as gentle nudges, guiding your thoughts to areas of your mind that hold emotions, memories, dreams, and even challenges. They offer a structured way to navigate your thoughts, especially when you're seeking clarity and peace of mind.

There are 101 journal prompts for you to review. . Don't feel obligated to follow them in sequence. These prompts are thought starters. Choose what feels right for the moment.

Here are 4 tips to get started:

○ **Tune Into Your Feelings**

• Scan through the list and pick a prompt that resonates with your current emotions or state of mind.

□ If a particular question or statement tugs at your heart or mind, begin there.

○ **Revisit When Needed**

• Your feelings and perspectives can change over time. It's perfectly okay to come back to the same prompt on different days.

□ Each revisit can shine light on a new facet of your feelings or experiences.

○ **Pressure-Free Zone**

• This isn't an exam; there are no right or wrong answers

□ They're tools designed to help you express and explore, Whether you write a sentence or fill pages, it's all valuable.

○ **Healing Through Discovery**

• By engaging with these prompts, you might un-cover feelings or memories you weren't actively aware of.

☐ Embrace these moments of discovery. They can be instrumental in your journey to better mental health.

As you consider the prompts in *J.O.U.R.N.A.L*, remember that they can help you in exploring your thoughts and emotions. These journal prompts are here to guide and inspire, but the real magic happens when you allow yourself to freely express and reflect. Your mental well-being is a journey, and every word you write down is a step towards a healthier, more self-aware you. Embrace the process.

J-Journey

A journey is more than just the act of moving from one place to another; it can be described as an exploration of self, an unfolding narrative of personal growth and discovery. It's understanding that the steps we take are often more significant than the destination we aim for. Along the way, we may encounter challenges, emotions, and revelations that shape our character and mold our perspectives. Each journey, whether physical or emotional, offers an opportunity to learn lessons that enrich us and broaden our horizons. Every person's journey is unique, filled with experiences and decisions. Embracing life's journey means valuing both the highs and the lows, the good and the not-so-good, understanding that each twist and turn contributes to the story of our life that is being defined each day. Leaders who appreciate the concept of a journey can guide others with patience, insight, and empathy, recognizing that the path traveled is just as, if not more, meaningful than any end goal. When you are on a journey, consider it a call to action, to be present, to appreciate each moment, and to uncover the lessons hidden within every step.

1. Reflect on a significant moment in your leadership journey. How has it shaped you?
2. What does the word journey mean to you, and how does it resonate with your life?
3. Write about someone who has positively impacted your journey.
4. How do you maintain perspective and stay focused on your unique journey?
5. Detail a challenge you faced in your journey and how you overcame it.
6. What are the values that guide your journey, and why are they important?
7. Explore a part of your journey that you once took for granted but now see its value.
8. How do you envision the next phase of your journey? What steps will you take to get there?
9. Write about a time when your journey took an unexpected turn, and what you learned.
10. What practices or habits do you implement to make your journey more fulfilling?

O - Optimism

Optimism is more than just seeing the glass as half full; it's about believing in yourself, trusting the process, and knowing that even in adversity, there is a lesson to be learned. It's this very optimism that serves as a catalyst for change and drives us towards brighter futures.

Reflections on OPTIMISM

1. True optimism isn't blind to challenges; it sees through them.
2. With optimism, every obstacle becomes an opportunity in disguise.
3. Optimism is the heartbeat of resilience, the voice that whispers, Try again.
4. An optimistic leader not only lifts themselves but raises the spirits of those they lead.
5. Every sunrise brings a promise, and with optimism, we embrace it wholeheartedly.
6. The flame of optimism has the power to light up the darkest rooms of doubt.
7. In the symphony of life, optimism provides the hopeful melody.
8. Through the lens of optimism, even setbacks are steps forward.
9. Optimism is a choice, a powerful one, that shapes our experiences and outcomes.

10. Nurture optimism, for it's the compass that points to endless possibilities.

Affirmations for OPTIMISM

1. I radiate optimism and inspire those around me.
2. Every situation holds a silver lining, and I choose to see it.
3. My optimism is the foundation of my strength and resilience.
4. With an optimistic heart, I attract positivity and opportunity.
5. I trust the journey, knowing my optimism guides me.
6. Challenges are temporary; my optimism is constant.
7. Through optimism, I transform barriers into bridges.
8. My future is always bright because I view it with optimism.
9. I lead with hope, knowing optimism is the key to inspiration.
10. I celebrate life daily and my optimism allows me to continue to thrive.

Journal Prompts for OPTIMISM

1. Describe a moment when optimism changed the course of a challenging situation.
2. How do you cultivate optimism in your daily life?
3. Write about a leader whose optimism has greatly influenced you.
4. How do you sustain your optimism during unforeseen challenges?
5. Envision an optimistic future for yourself. What does it look like?
6. How has optimism shaped your leadership journey?
7. Reflect on a time when someone else's optimism uplifted and encouraged you.
8. How do you encourage optimism in your team or community?
9. What barriers to optimism have you encountered, and how did you overcome them?
10. How does optimism impact your decision-making process?

U - Understanding

Understanding is more than just comprehension; it's a deep-seated wisdom that touches our very core. It's recognizing the interconnectedness of our lives, acknowledging the bigger picture, and placing ourselves within that vast tapestry. Every one of us faces moments where we might not feel our best or understand our purpose, and during these times, it becomes important to discern our feelings, seek guidance, and confide in those we trust. This type of understanding paves the way for genuine knowledge, compassion, and empathy. Leaders with this form of understanding can foster communities rooted in trust, respect, and mutual growth. This requires us to look beyond ourselves, urging us to comprehend not just our own experiences, but those of the world around us.

Reflections on UNDERSTANDING

1. True understanding is seeing with the heart, not just the eyes.
2. With understanding comes the realization of our shared human experience.
3. Leadership is understanding that every individual is a part of a larger narrative.
4. Through genuine understanding, we embrace both joys and tribulations as integral parts of life's journey.

5. Understanding is the foundation upon which compassion is built.

6. To understand another's journey is to open a gateway to deeper connections.

7. Wisdom begins with understanding; it's the first step to true enlightenment.

8. Understanding is not merely about knowing but truly connecting with the essence of matters.

9. True leadership thrives on mutual understanding and respect.

10. Everyone has a story; understanding that story is where transformation begins.

Affirmations for UNDERSTANDING

1. Understanding is my superpower; it lights up my path forward.
2. Every moment of understanding brings me closer to my true self.
3. By seeking to understand, I unlock doors to endless possibilities.
4. I am patient with myself, knowing that understanding grows over time.
5. I am unstoppable because I seek to understand.
6. Every effort I make to understand deepens my connection to the world.
7. With understanding, I transform obstacles into stepping stones.
8. Understanding myself is the foundation of my strength and confidence.
9. I am committed to understanding others, and in turn, enriching my own journey.
10. Every day, my quest for understanding adds value to my life's purpose.

Journal Prompts for UNDERSTANDING

1. Recall a moment when you felt deeply understood. How did it transform your perspective?
2. How do you ensure you're connecting to the deeper stories of those around you?
3. Describe a time when understanding someone's experience reshaped your view on an issue.

4. How do you foster a space where everyone feels understood and valued?

5. What practices help you cultivate a deeper understanding of the world and its intricacies?

6. Share an instance where you had to step out of your comfort zone to understand another's viewpoint.

7. How do you reconcile misunderstandings, ensuring they lead to growth?

8. In what ways have you evolved in your understanding over the years?

9. What challenges have you faced in your journey to understanding and how have they shaped you?

10. How does your understanding influence the daily choices and decisions you make?

R - Reflection

At the core of growth is the act of reflection. By looking inward, we gain insights that help us our path forward. Reflection serves as a mirror, revealing not just our actions but the intentions and motivations behind them. It's an opportunity to pause, analyze, and recalibrate. For leaders, the ability to reflect translates to understanding the greater narrative, recognizing the nuances, and fostering an environment of continuous improvement. Taking time to look internally for self-reflection allows for a broader understanding of the world around us, ensuring that as we move forward, we do so with clarity, purpose, and compassion.

Reflections on REFLECTION

1. In the mirror of reflection, clarity emerges from the shadows.
2. By revisiting our past, we set ourselves up for a more enlightened future.
3. Every moment of introspection is a step closer to our authentic self.
4. Reflection transforms experience into wisdom.
5. In stillness, we find answers that elude us in the chaos.
6. To reflect is to engage in an intimate conversation with oneself.

7. Leaders grow not just by action, but by pausing to reflect on those actions.
8. Through reflection, we gain the foresight to navigate tomorrow's uncertainties.
9. To reflect upon our journey is to better understand our destination.
10. Life's lessons often reveal themselves in moments of quiet reflection.

Affirmations for REFLECTION

1. I embrace reflection as the guiding my journey.
2. Every introspective moment enriches my soul and broadens my horizon.
3. I value the lessons that emerge from the depths of reflection.
4. In my moments of stillness, I discover my truest intentions.
5. I trust the process of looking inward to lead me forward.
6. My path is illuminated by the insights I gain from reflecting.
7. Each day, I commit to understanding myself a little more.
8. I cherish the wisdom that reflection brings into my life.
9. My leadership is enhanced by my commitment to self -awareness.
10. In reflection, I find peace, purpose, and direction.

Journal Prompts for REFLECTION

1. Think of a recent challenge you faced. What insights did you gain upon reflecting on it?

2. How do you make time for reflection amidst your busy schedule?

3. Describe an instance when reflection changed a decision you were about to make.

4. How has the practice of introspection changed your relationships with others?

5. What tools or practices assist you in deepening your reflective moments?

6. Share a valuable lesson you've learned solely through the act of reflection.

7. How do you differentiate between being reflective and being overly critical of yourself?

8. In what ways has reflection played a role in your personal growth journey?

9. How do you translate your reflective insights into actionable steps?

10. Describe a moment of reflection that led to a significant personal or professional breakthrough.

N - Nurturing

Nurturing is about caring, growth, and fostering positive development. Whether it's nurturing oneself or others, this principle represents a commitment to continual growth, empathy, compassion, and love. In leadership, nurturing involves mentoring, inspiring, and investing time and energy into personal and team development. The power of nurturing lies in its ability to cultivate potential, build resilience, and form lasting connections. It encourages us to embrace the journey with a sense of purpose and fulfillment. This is about more than just support; it's about recognizing potential and acting to help it blossom.

Reflections on NURTURING

1. Nurturing seeds of potential leads to a garden of success.
2. The art of nurturing is found in the balance of patience, understanding, and love.
3. Nurturing others begins with nurturing oneself.
4. True leadership is found in the gentle art of nurturing growth.
5. In every act of nurturing, we are planting the seeds of positive change.
6. Nurturing is the bridge between knowing potential and realizing it.

7. Fostering growth requires the loving attention of a nurturing heart.
8. A nurturing environment is where dreams find the soil to grow.
9. Through nurturing, we cultivate not just growth but lifelong connections.
10. Every act of nurturing is a step towards a brighter, more compassionate world.

Affirmations for NURTURING

1. I nurture myself and others with love, respect, and understanding.
2. Every day, I commit to fostering growth in myself and those around me.
3. I transform potential into achievement.
4. In my leadership, I embrace the role of a mentor, guiding with compassion.
5. I recognize the potential in others and act to help it flourish.
6. My actions and words reflect a commitment to nurturing success.
7. I find joy in the growth that comes from nurturing.
8. Through empathy and patience, I create a nurturing environment.
9. My heart is open, and my actions are aligned with nurturing growth.
10. Nurturing others enriches my life and strengthens my connections.

Journal Prompts for NURTURING

1. Describe a time when you felt nurtured. How did it impact your growth?

2. How do you ensure that you are nurturing yourself as well as others?

3. What does a nurturing environment look like to you?

4. Share an experience where you played a nurturing role in someone's development.

5. How can you integrate more nurturing behaviors into your leadership?

6. What are some barriers you've faced in nurturing yourself or others? How did you overcome them?

7. Describe a mentor who nurtured your growth. What did you learn from them?

8. How does nurturing others affect your own well-being and growth?

9. What strategies do you use to nurture positive relationships with your team or family?

10. Reflect on how nurturing connects with other principles like understanding, reflection, and acceptance in your life.

A - Acceptance

Acceptance is a powerful tool for growth. It's the realization that we don't have to be perfect, that it's okay to have flaws and make mistakes. By embracing acceptance, we recognize our limitations and also our potential. In leadership, acceptance is about understanding the diverse backgrounds, strengths, and challenges of those you lead. It's about creating an inclusive environment where every individual feels valued and heard. Acceptance is not just about passivity but about actively embracing the entirety of a situation or a person, including oneself.

Reflections on ACCEPTANCE

1. In acceptance, we find the freedom to be our authentic selves.
2. True leadership flourishes in an environment of acceptance and inclusion.
3. By embracing acceptance, we pave the way for transformative growth.
4. Acceptance isn't about resignation, but about recognizing reality and choosing to thrive within it.
5. The beauty of diversity shines brightest in the light of acceptance.
6. Every act of acceptance is a step towards a more inclusive world.

7. Accepting oneself is the foundation upon which we can genuinely accept others.

8. In the heart of acceptance lies boundless potential for connection.

9. Every challenge, when accepted, becomes an opportunity for growth.

10. Acceptance is the bridge between understanding and action.

Affirmations for ACCEPTANCE

1. I choose to embrace acceptance in every aspect of my life.

2. By accepting myself, I strengthen my capacity to accept others.

3. Every day, I celebrate the diversity and potential in those around me.

4. My leadership is enriched by my commitment to inclusive acceptance.

5. Through acceptance, I discover the strength within my vulnerabilities.

6. I value and honor the unique experiences and perspectives of every individual.

7. My actions radiate acceptance, fostering trust and collaboration.

8. In every challenge, I find the opportunity by choosing acceptance.

9. Acceptance empowers me to navigate life with grace and resilience.

10. I am dedicated to building a world where acceptance is the cornerstone of every interaction.

Journal Prompts for ACCEPTANCE

1. Reflect on a moment when acceptance played a pivotal role in your personal or professional life.
2. How do you cultivate an environment of acceptance in your leadership?
3. What challenges have you faced in your journey towards self-acceptance?
4. Describe a time when embracing acceptance led to a positive outcome in a difficult situation.
5. How does acceptance influence your relationships with those around you?
6. Share an instance when someone's acceptance had an impact on you.
7. How do you reconcile acceptance with the desire for change and improvement?
8. What are the barriers to acceptance, both self and of others? How do you navigate them?
9. Reflect on the interplay between understanding, nurturing, and acceptance in your life.
10. Describe an actionable step you can take to promote a deeper sense of acceptance in your community or organization.

L - Love

Love is more than just an emotion; it's a force that can drive positive change, inspire profound connections, and provide solace in moments of adversity. Leaders who lead with love are not just admired, but they also create environments where trust and loyalty flourish. Love extends beyond just relationships; it's about self-love, respect for all living beings, and a genuine appreciation for the world around us. It's about recognizing the value in every person and every moment.

Reflections on LOVE

1. Love, in its truest form, knows no bounds and recognizes no barriers.
2. To lead with love is to lead with an open heart and an open mind.
3. Love is the anchor that keeps us grounded, and the wind that pushes us forward.
4. In love, we discover our capacity for resilience, forgiveness, and growth.
5. Love has the power to heal wounds, bridge divides, and inspire great endeavors.
6. Self-love is the starting point of all other loves and the foundation for genuine leadership.
7. Love is the silent language that every heart understands and every soul seeks.

8. In the embrace of love, we find the strength to face our greatest challenges.
9. Love can guide us through life's darkest nights and brightest days.
10. True leadership can be observed from a heart filled with love and compassion.
11. Love is both the journey and the destination, enriching every step we take.

Affirmations for LOVE

1. I lead with love, creating an environment of trust and understanding.
2. Every day, I make the conscious choice to approach life with love and compassion.
3. My capacity to love myself strengthens my capacity to love others.
4. Love guides my decisions, connections and bridging differences.
5. I recognize and cherish the love present in every moment and every interaction.
6. Through love, I see the value and potential in every individual.
7. My love is a source of strength, healing, and inspiration for myself and those around me.
8. Love empowers me to face challenges with grace and resilience.
9. I am dedicated to spreading love, understanding, and positivity wherever I go.

10. My heart remains open, receptive, and loving in all situations.

11. Through the lens of love, I see a world filled with endless possibilities.

Journal Prompts for LOVE

1. Reflect on a moment where love played a transformative role in your life.

2. How do you ensure that love remains a guiding principle in your leadership style?

3. Describe a time when leading with love resulted in a positive change.

4. Describe your journey towards self-love and the challenges you encountered along the way.

5. How does love influence your relationships with colleagues, friends, and family?

6. Recall a time when you felt genuinely loved and appreciated. How did that make you feel?

7. What does it mean to you to lead with love, especially in challenging situations?

8. How do you foster an environment where love, trust, and mutual respect thrive?

9. Explore the connection between love, acceptance, and understanding in your life.

10. Reflect on the actions you can take to promote love in your community or organization.

11. Describe a lesson you've learned about love, its challenges, and its rewards.

Journey

_____

_____

_____

_____

_____

_____

_____

_____

_____

_____

_____

_____

_____

_____

_____

_____

_____

_____

_____

_____

_____

_____

Optimism

_____

_____

_____

_____

_____

_____

_____

_____

_____

_____

_____

_____

_____

_____

_____

_____

_____

_____

_____

_____

_____

_____

_____

Understanding

_____

_____

_____

_____

_____

_____

_____

_____

_____

_____

_____

_____

_____

_____

_____

_____

_____

_____

_____

_____

_____

_____

_____

Reflection

_____

_____

_____

_____

_____

_____

_____

_____

_____

_____

_____

_____

_____

_____

_____

_____

_____

_____

_____

_____

_____

_____

_____

Nurturing

_____

_____

_____

_____

_____

_____

_____

_____

_____

_____

_____

_____

_____

_____

_____

_____

_____

_____

_____

_____

_____

_____

_____

_____

_____

Acceptance

_____

_____

_____

_____

_____

_____

_____

_____

_____

_____

_____

_____

_____

_____

_____

_____

_____

_____

_____

_____

_____

_____

Love

_____

_____

_____

_____

_____

_____

_____

_____

_____

_____

_____

_____

_____

_____

_____

_____

_____

_____

_____

_____

_____

_____

Mindful Moments in the J.O.U.R.N.A.L. Journey

Introduction: The Essence of Mindfulness

Mindfulness is the act of being deeply present and engaged in the current moment, without distraction or judgment. It's about appreciating the "here and now" and embracing each experience without trying to change it. Why does mindfulness matter? By grounding ourselves in the present, we can reduce anxiety, increase our emotional intelligence, and foster a profound sense of well-being. While mindfulness might often be associated with meditation, it takes on various shapes and forms, including simple daily exercises. This chapter presents a series of mindfulness exercises that align with our J.O.U.R.N.A.L. journey.

1. Journey of Optimism
Positive Affirmation Breathing

Objective: To instill a sense of hope and positivity.

Exercise:

·   Find a quiet space to sit or lie down.

·   Close your eyes and take deep breaths.

·   As you breathe in, think of a positive affirmation like "I am hopeful."

·   As you breathe out, let go of any negative thoughts.

·   Repeat for 5-10 minutes.

2. Understanding
Sensory Awareness

Objective: To enhance your understanding of the present moment and your surroundings.

Exercise:

·   Sit in a comfortable position.

·   Close your eyes and focus on your five senses.

·   Identify one thing you can hear, one you can feel, one you can smell, and so on.

·   This exercise helps ground you in the present and cultivates a deeper understanding of the moment.

3. Reflection
Mirror Exercise

Objective: To develop self-awareness and self-appreciation.

Exercise:
- Stand in front of a mirror.
- Look deeply into your own eyes.
- Think about your achievements, challenges, and growth.
- Whisper positive affirmations to yourself, appreciating your journey.

4. Nurturing

Self-Hug

Objective: To provide self-care and self-love.

Exercise:
- Sit comfortably.
- Wrap your arms around yourself, giving yourself a gentle hug.
- Breathe deeply and feel the warmth and comfort.
- Remind yourself that you deserve love and care.

5. Acceptance

Floating Leaves on a Stream

Objective: To cultivate acceptance of thoughts and feelings without judgment.

Exercise:
- Close your eyes and imagine a serene stream.
- Visualize leaves floating on the water's surface.
- Place each of your thoughts or feelings on these leaves.

- Let them float by without judgment, accepting each one as it comes and goes.

6. Love
Heartbeat Meditation

Objective: To foster self-love and connection.

Exercise:

- Sit or lie down in a quiet place.
- Place your hand over your heart.
- Feel its beat, its rhythm.
- Recognize it as a sign of life, of love, and of existence.
- Think about things you love about yourself and the love you have to give to others.

7. Peaceful Pondering

Objective: To nurture peaceful reflection on daily experiences.

Exercise:

- Find a quiet corner.
- Reflect on a positive experience from the day.
- Ponder on what made it special, how it made you feel, and its impact on your day.

8. Guided Imagery
Safe Haven

Objective: To create a mental space of safety and tranquility.

Exercise:

· Close your eyes and envision a place where you feel most at peace.

· It could be a beach, forest, or even a childhood home.

· Walk through this place, engage with the surroundings, and absorb the serenity.

9. Body Scan

Objective: To foster awareness and appreciation for every part of your body.

Exercise:

· Lie down and close your eyes.

· Mentally scan your body from your toes to your head.

· Thank each part for its function and send it love.

10. Mindful Eating

Objective: To enhance gratitude and pleasure in daily tasks.

Exercise:

· Choose a meal or snack.

· Eat it slowly, savoring every flavor, texture, and aroma.

· Reflect on the journey of the food and express gratitude for the nourishment.

11. Gratitude Gaze

Objective: To cultivate a sense of gratitude.

Exercise:

· Find a window or sit outdoors.

· Gaze by looking at the sky, trees, or surroundings.

· Reflect on three things you're grateful for in that moment.

12. Sound Immersion

Objective: To develop a deeper connection with the ambient sounds.

Exercise:

· Close your eyes and focus on the various sounds around you.

· Instead of labeling the sounds, immerse yourself in the experience of listening.

13. Emotion Surfing

Objective: To understand and acknowledge emotions without judgment.

Exercise:

· Find a quiet spot and close your eyes.

· Recognize any emotion you're feeling at the moment, whether it's joy, anger, sadness, or anything else.

- Instead of reacting, just observe the emotion. Imagine it as a wave, and you're simply surfing on it, witnessing its rise and fall.

14. Five Senses Awareness

Objective: To connect deeply with the present moment.

Exercise:

- Sit comfortably and close your eyes.
- One by one, focus on each of your five senses. What can you hear, touch, smell, taste, and see (even with your eyes closed)?
- Spend a minute or two on each sense, fully immersing yourself in the experience.

15. Compassionate Breathing

Objective: To nurture feelings of love and compassion.

Exercise:

- Sit or lie down comfortably.
- Inhale deeply, imagining love and warmth filling you. As you exhale, envision spreading that love and warmth to those around you.
- With each breath, let the feelings of compassion grow.

16. Anchoring with Touch

Objective: To ground yourself in the present.

Exercise:

- Touch an object near you. It could be a desk, a cup, a piece of fabric, or anything else.
- Fully feel the texture, temperature, and shape of the object.
- Let the object anchor you to the present moment, pushing away any distracting thoughts.

17. Movement and Stretch

Objective: To connect mindfully with your body.

Exercise:

- Stand up and stretch your body.
- Pay close attention to each muscle as you stretch, feeling where tension is released and where it remains.
- Move slowly and with intention, whether it's a simple stretch or a full-body movement.

18. Loving-kindness Meditation

Objective: To cultivate feelings of goodwill and kindness.

Exercise:

- Close your eyes and take a few deep breaths.
- Think of someone you care about deeply. Send them wishes of love, happiness, and well-being.

· Slowly expand these wishes to acquaintances, strangers, and even people you may have conflicts with.

19. Nature Connection

Objective: To feel interconnectedness with the world.

Exercise:

· Spend some time outdoors, whether it's in a park, garden, or forest.

· Sit and observe the natural processes around you: the rustling of leaves, the chirping of birds, or the flow of water.

· Feel your own existence as part of this beautiful web of life.

20. Mindful Walking

Objective: To ground oneself through deliberate movement.

Exercise:

· Choose a quiet path or area.

· Walk slowly, feeling each step as your foot touches the ground and lifts again.

· Sync your breathing with your steps, inhaling for a certain number of steps, then exhaling for the same count.

Mindfulness:
A Toolkit for Your Mental Health Journey

With the **20** mindfulness exercises provided, you have a set of tools ready for use. Each exercise offers a different pathway to peace, insight, and a deeper understanding of oneself. These practices are designed to enhance your connection to the present moment, bringing clarity and calm into your daily life. Whether you're exploring these exercises on your own or sharing them in a group setting, there can be many benefits.

Incorporating Mindfulness into Your Daily Life

As you've explored these introductory exercises, the power of mindfulness may become more evident. Like mastering any skill, its impact grows with consistent practice. These exercises can easily fit into your daily routine, whether you're seeking:

A Moment of Calm

In the middle of a busy day, mindfulness can be your haven of peace.

Connection with Others

Use these exercises as icebreakers or group activities, fostering meaningful interactions.

Enhanced Self-Awareness

Take a moment to reflect and understand yourself better with each practice. This can be particularly beneficial in moments of decision-making, when trying to understand one's feelings, or when navigating complex personal challenges.

Morning Routine

Begin your day with a grounding exercise, setting a peaceful tone for the hours ahead.

Work Breaks

Take a few minutes during your workday, especially when transitioning between tasks, to re-center and refocus.

Before Bed

Ease into sleep by letting go of the day's stresses and entering a state of relaxation.

Conflict Resolution

Before addressing a disagreement or misunderstanding, take a few moments for mindfulness. This can help in approaching the situation with clarity and empathy.

Before Big Decisions

If you're on the verge of making a significant choice, a mindfulness exercise can assist in clearing mental clutter, aiding in better judgment.

Social Settings

Before entering a social event or gathering, a quick mindfulness practice can help you be present and enjoy the company of others.

Learning Environments

Whether you're a student or attending a workshop, a moment of mindfulness can enhance concentration and retention.

Physical Activity

Pairing mindfulness with activities like walking, jogging, or stretching can heighten the experience and its benefits.

Dealing with Negative Emotions

When feelings of sadness, anger, or frustration arise, use mindfulness to acknowledge and process these emotions without being overwhelmed by them.

Celebratory Moments

During joyful and celebratory occasions, mindfulness can help in deepening the appreciation and immersion in the moment.

Remember, the power of mindfulness lies not just in practicing it but in recognizing its potential to enhance various moments in your life.

∞

How to Integrate Mindfulness

Frequency

Aim for at least one exercise daily. With time, the principles of mindfulness will become a natural part of your daily thoughts and actions.

Usage: Consider ways that you can use them.

Alone

Perfect for introspection and personal growth.

In Groups

A fresh way to bond and engage at a deeper level.

De-stress

When life feels too much, a short mindfulness exercise can refresh and ground you.

Start of Day

Begin each morning with a mindfulness practice to set a positive and focused tone for the day.

Meal Times

Before eating, take a moment to be present with your food. Appreciate its colors, textures, and scents.

While Commuting

Make commute times an opportunity for grounding.

Exercise

Integrate mindfulness to elevate the benefits of physical activity.

Challenging Tasks

Use mindfulness to aid focus and clarity before tackling difficult tasks.

Creative Processes

Enhance creativity during artistic endeavors.

Before Meetings

Be more present, attentive, and effective during discussions.

Transitions

Use mindfulness as a mental 'buffer' between tasks.

Nature Walks

Absorb your environment while outdoors.

Listening to Music

Engage deeply with the rhythm, instruments, and lyrics.

End of Day

Reflect on the day and set intentions for the next.

When Anxious

Use mindfulness to manage and understand strong emotions.

Reading

Enhance comprehension and enjoyment with mindfulness before engaging with a book or article.

Before Social Engagements

Use mindfulness to be more present and relaxed during social activities.

Learning & Studying

Boost concentration and retention during academic endeavors.

While Waiting

Turn waiting times into opportunities for mindfulness.

Before Digital Activity

Set a focused and intentional tone before browsing the internet or engaging with digital platforms.

Household Chores

Engage fully with everyday tasks like washing dishes, cleaning, or gardening.

Shopping

Use mindfulness to reflect on your true needs and intentions before making a purchase.

Problem Solving

Approach solutions with clarity and creativity after a mindfulness break.

With the mindfulness exercises and techniques you've explored, you now possess powerful tools to be present, engaged, and deeply connected to each moment. Mindfulness is more than just a practice; it's a way of living, a path to being fully attuned to life's experiences, whether they are moments of joy, challenge, or everyday happenings.

Remember this is not just a book—it's a space where moments can be captured and reflected upon. As you continue to incorporate mindfulness in your daily life, let your J.O.U.R.N.A.L be the place where your insights, feelings, and revelations find a home. Remember, being present isn't just about noticing the moment; it's about understanding, embracing, and growing from each experience.

Mapping Your Mental Health Journey

Early in my career, I served as an occupational therapist in behavioral health units, catering to both inpatient hospitalizations and outpatient partial hospitalization programs. Whether working with youth or adults, I consistently recognized a need to map their mental health journey. This observation was further reinforced during my time as a guidance counselor with a K-12 endorsement. In this chapter, there are a variety of activities for your mental health toolkit. As we navigate the complexities of everyday life, taking moments to check in on our mental state becomes important. This chapter provides practical tools that empower you to actively monitor, reflect on, and understand the ebb and flow of your mental health journey. By engaging in these activities, you'll unlock deeper self-awareness, allowing you to celebrate the highs, learn from the lows, and shape a path toward continuous growth and well-being.

Progress Tracking

Activity: Dedicate a specific time, perhaps the last Sunday of every month, for a mental health check-in. During this session, reflect on the moments that defined the month, the lessons learned, and set intentions for the days ahead.

Why: These regular introspections provide snapshots of your evolving mental state, offering both a rearview mirror to see how far you've come and a compass pointing towards future growth.

Mood Tracking

Activity: Design or print a mood calendar, adding colors or symbols that represent different emotions. At the end of each day, fill in the calendar based on how you felt overall.

Why: Visualizing your emotional landscape allows you to pinpoint specific patterns and triggers, granting a clearer picture of the factors that elevate or dampen your mood.

Gratitude Journaling

Activity: Before bed each night, jot down three events or moments from the day that filled you with gratitude.

Why: This practice refocuses your mind on life's positives, serving as a daily reminder of the beauty and goodness surrounding you, even during challenging periods.

Affirmation Crafting

Activity: Develop a list of positive affirmations, ensuring they align with your goals and values. Make it a habit to read through them every morning or during moments of doubt.

Why: These affirmations become personal mantras, bolstering your confidence and reinforcing positivity, ensuring you tackle challenges with a robust mindset.

Mind-Body Connection

Activity: Choose a physical activity—whether it's a morning walk, a midday stretch, or an evening yoga session. As you move, pay close attention to each motion, grounding yourself in the experience.

Why: Pairing physical activity with conscious presence benefits both body and mind. This synergy can lead to reduced anxiety levels, heightened focus, and an overall sense of tranquility.

Emotion Visualization

Activity: Find a quiet space, close your eyes, and envision your emotions as colors or landscapes. See them, acknowledge them, and let them flow without judgment.

Why: By giving form to feelings, you create a safe space to understand and process them, leading to better emotional management and balance.

Personal Strengths Inventory

Activity: Create a list of your strengths and achievements. Update it when you accomplish something new or recognize another strength.

Why: Regularly acknowledging and celebrating your abilities fosters self-confidence and provides motivation during times when you might feel stuck or low.

Daily Intention Setting

Activity: Start each day by setting a clear intention. Whether it's to remain calm in stressful situations, to listen actively, or to prioritize self-care, keep this intention in mind throughout the day.

Why: Intentions act as guiding lights, shaping your actions, decisions, and interactions, helping to mold a purpose-driven day.

Letter to Future Self

Activity: Write a letter to your future self, outlining your hopes, dreams, fears, and current state. Seal it and set a date to open it in the future.

Why: This activity serves as a time capsule of your feelings, allowing you to reflect on your growth and changes in perspective over time.

Guided Imagery

Activity: Find or create a guided imagery script. Close your eyes and let the narrative transport you to a peaceful place, focusing solely on the experience.

Why: This relaxation technique reduces stress, calms the mind, and can offer momentary escapes from daily pressures.

Your mental health journey is uniquely yours, filled with its distinctive moments, lessons, and turning points. Through the tools provided in this chapter, you're not just passively experiencing the journey but actively shaping, understanding, and cherishing it. As you utilize these tools, know that every reflection, every noted emotion, and every positive affirmation helps in carving a path that's part self-awareness and purpose. This is your journey and the possibilities are endless.

Conclusion

Honoring the Process

Life unfolds in chapters, moments of clarity, periods of challenge, and intervals of revelation. Each phase tells a story, revealing the beauty of struggle, the melody of triumph, and the wisdom of introspection. As you turned the pages of this book, you were invited into a realm of reflection, optimism, and a deeper understanding of self.

This book has hopefully provided you with a lot of different tools, like a menu to provide resources that can empower, inspire, and elevate you. Remember life is not just about experiencing situations that we find difficult, you must have purpose. Taking time to acknowledge your emotions, reflect on life's moments, and embrace change are important steps to explore. In doing so, you develop strategies for the promotion of good mental health and well-being.

As you come to the end of this reading, consider it not as a conclusion but as a checkpoint on your ongoing adventure in life. Take the insights gained and spread lessons you learned with others. Your journey, with its unique challenges and victories, is a testament to the enduring human spirit. You can do it. You matter. You have a purpose.

Dr. Katherine Y. Brown

May your path always be illuminated by moments of self-care, by the joy you cultivate, and by the peace you choose daily, leading you to a life of purpose and fulfillment.

In the quiet corners of our days, where we find joy, where we honor ourselves, there lies the true essence of growth. Protect your peace, prioritize what replenishes you, and always remember to honor the journey of your mental health.

- Dr. Katherine Y. Brown

149

Bonus Content

Making More of Your Journaling

The journey of self-discovery can be both exciting and enlightening. When you journal you're creating a book, documentation of your story, it's a tool and a mirror. While it's a personal space for reflection, it can also be a lively topic of discussion, a means to connect with others, and a guide for group activities.

Writing in a journal often starts as something we do alone. But when we share it with others, it can help us get closer, learn new things, and understand each other better. In this bonus section, there are activities and ideas for engagement. These can help friends, classmates, or team members connect in new ways.

Teachers, group leaders, or anyone who loves journaling can use these activities to bring people together. Picture classrooms filled with shared stories, group meetings that start with deep questions, or friends learning more about each other. There are so many things you can do with a journal!

1. **Host a Journal Party:** Get a group together, ensuring everyone has their own copy of this book. Spend some time writing individually, and then, if comfortable, share your reflections. Use the opportunity to learn from each other's insights and experiences.

2. **Topic Group Discussion:** Choose a theme from this book and discuss it in a group setting. This can be done in a classroom, community center, or even informally amongst friends. Discussing a common topic from different perspectives enriches understanding.

3. **Book Club Approach:** Like a traditional book club, gather people at regular intervals to discuss what they've written or discovered in their journals. Each member can choose a particular entry or prompt they want to discuss, fostering deeper understanding and providing support in the journey of self-discovery.

4. **Ice Breakers & Leadership Programs:** Use journal prompts as ice breakers for group activities, workshops, or team-building exercises. Pick a prompt and let everyone answer it briefly, kickstarting discussions and getting to know one another.

5. **Classroom Connections:** Educators can use journal prompts for class discussions, group projects, or assignments. It helps students think more deeply about topics and can improve their writing skills.

6. **Digital Journal Groups:** Create a digital group using the online platform of your choice. Allow people to share and discuss their journal entries. This can add a modern twist to the practice of journaling.

7. **Guided Group Sessions:** Organize sessions where a leader or facilitator chooses a prompt and guides participants through it, followed by group discussions. This is a great way for newcomers to journaling to begin.

Personal Growth Workshops: Organize workshops focusing on personal development, using this book as a foundation. Participants can explore topics in-depth and set actionable goals based on their reflections.

As you make use of this book and engage with these activities, remember it's not only about understanding yourself but also connecting and understanding others. **Keep writing, keep sharing, and keep discovering the stories that unite us all.**